THE NEW EVANGELISM

☆ ☆ ☆

Alan Walker

Abingdon

Nashville

THE NEW EVANGELISM

Copyright © 1975 by Abingdon Press

Library of Congress Cataloging in Publication Data

WALKER, ALAN, 1911-   The new evangelism.
1. Evangelistic work. I. Title.   *112p.; 19cm.*
BV3790.W314   269'.2   74-28016

ISBN 0-687-27736-1

Scripture quotations unless otherwise noted are from the Revised Standard Version of the Bible, copyrighted 1946, 1952, and 1971, by the Division of Christian Education, National Council of Churches, and are used by permission.

The poems "Poverty" and "Where I'll Find You" are from Ken Walsh's *Sometime I Weep,* copyright © 1973, SCM Press Ltd.

MANUFACTURED BY THE PARTHENON PRESS AT
NASHVILLE, TENNESSEE, UNITED STATES OF AMERICA

CONTENTS

THE MOTIVE FOR MISSION

The time is overdue for Christians to find a new, saner, larger evangelism. The new evangelism must express the fruits of biblical scholarship and appeal to the mind as well as the emotions of modern people. It must draw together the personal and social elements of the gospel, seeking at the same time the conversion of men and women and the building of a society fit for people to live in.

"The missionary era is over, and the era of world mission has begun," said Emilio Castro at the Bangkok Christian Conference. The amazing missionary era of the last two hundred years was God's strategy for placing the church in every continent and island. Out of this vast missionary outreach have come indigenous churches established and ready for the next great worldwide Christian advance. Out of it has emerged what Archbishop Temple called "the great new fact of our time," the ecumenical movement. Now we are able to see in new ways the vision of Jesus when he said that the field is the world.

The world is crying out today for a Christian resurgence. The missionary imperative is as urgent as ever.

There can be no more receiving and sending churches as in the nineteenth century. There can be no assumed superiority of a Western world over the rest of the earth. The Western world is underdeveloped morally and spiritually, as poorer nations are underdeveloped physically. Christians are called to share together in the one world task of offering Jesus Christ to all people.

The need of the world for the good news of Jesus is as great as ever. Nothing has happened in secular advance which has outstripped the world's need of Christ. Rapid social change is little more than the moving around of the scenery of life. The essential drama of living is enacted, be it in the life of the individual or in society as a whole. God is the same, the Christian gospel is the same, and man's fundamental needs remain the same.

A new factor is the population explosion. Two billion people are yet to learn of Christ and his salvation. As every generation must be confronted with the Christian story, the world's Christian forces are facing the greatest challenge that has confronted them since the first century. A new evangelism simply must be found for the new era of world mission that has dawned.

The New Motive

A new evangelism, expressed in terms of contemporary experience, must begin with finding a new motive for mission. The imperatives of earlier centuries, particularly of the nineteenth and the first half of the twentieth century, are no longer valid or compelling.

Dr. Michael Green states there was a three-fold motive

for mission in the early church. First, there was a sense of gratitude for what Christ had done. Second, early Christians were conscious of their responsibility to God to communicate the message they had received. Third, there was a concern, a passion for people.

As Dr. Green says in his book, *Evangelism in the Early Church* (London: Hodder & Stoughton, 1970), "There can be little doubt that the main motive for evangelism was a theological one. The disciples spread the Gospel because of the overwhelming experience of the love of God which they had received from Jesus Christ" (p. 236).

Over the years since the first century, the motive for mission has varied. Let us look for a moment at the evangelism of the eighteenth, nineteenth, and early twentieth centuries. It is necessary to understand the motive of these recent years, for it is still thrusting itself into the contemporary Christian scene. The driving motive of Christians in these years was a passion for souls. With the vivid belief in the reality of heaven and hell, Christians sought to rescue people from eternal punishment and to open the door of heaven for them before it was too late.

Perhaps the most vivid expression of this type of motive can be heard throbbing in the ministry of Dr. Jonathan Edwards. It is powerfully expressed in his famous sermon "Sinners in the Hands of an Angry God." Dr. Edwards apparently produced a tremendous impact on the eastern coast of America as he thundered: "God holds you over the pit of hell. You hang by a slender thread with the flames of divine wrath flashing about it. Now harken to the loud call of God's word and providence. Therefore let everyone who is out of Christ now awake and fly from the wrath to come."

This was not the sole motive of some of the best preaching of the period. As in the message of the famous evangelist Dr. C. G. Finney, there was a strong social conscience. Unfortunately as this period advanced, this larger vision of the gospel gradually declined until a more escapist theology predominated. Rather than struggling for the redemption of society, the passion for souls became a selfish, personal desire to avoid God's wrath.

Nineteenth-century motives for mission are no longer viable or credible. Enticement of heaven or the dread of hell no longer possess the power they once did. There are several reasons for this decline.

While the fear of death is a real factor in today's consciousness, death is not quite the same threat to humanity as it was when the mortality rate for children was high and when life expectancy was low, about twenty-eight or thirty years. Thus death was vividly encountered in family circles and in the community in ways not seen today. While sudden death on the roads or in the air remains possible, we all assume it will not happen to us. Therefore death has receded away into the distance; as a result, death's consequences appear less threatening.

In psychological theory concerning the rearing of children, the concept of behavior modification stemming from fear or the promise of reward is rejected. We are agreed that bribes or threats create unworthy motives for living. Therefore Christians are uneasy in summoning men and women to Jesus Christ on the basis of the attractiveness of heaven or the dread darkness of hell.

THE MOTIVE FOR MISSION

Many cannot comprehend the moment of dying with the tremendous significance that some forms of nineteenth-century theology attempted to relate. To impose this burden on the incident of death, be it early or late, seems almost to take out of the hands of God a man's or woman's eternal destiny and to place it in the hands of others. A boy of sixteen who has not yet come to an acceptance of the Christian position, though he may be moving toward it, is knocked down and killed by a drunken driver. Is his eternal destiny settled at that moment? If it is, if death carries this significance, then it would seem that the eternal fate of that boy was governed by the irresponsibility of one of his fellows.

The heaviest indictment against the nineteenth-century motive for mission lies in the concept of God which it presumed. The concept of hell as everlasting torment is in direct conflict with the whole Christian concept of God as love. Nineteenth-century preachers seemed sometimes to present God as being worse than Hitler. What kind of God is it who would create an eternal concentration camp from which there was no escape? This is not the God of justice and mercy revealed by Jesus Christ.

Many today, therefore, while recognizing many biblical passages which emphasize the finality of death, are hearing other strands of message through the Scriptures. Jesus told a parable in which he said the good shepherd seeks the lost sheep until he finds it. There is the strange passage in Peter about the risen Christ going to speak to the spirits in prison. There is the great, often-repeated declaration of the Scriptures saying that the mercy of God is everlasting. The judgments of God abound on

11

the earth, and the wages of sin are still death. Many modern Christians no longer find it possible to accept the fact that the motive for evangelism can be either the promise of heaven or the fear of hell.

What then is a new possible motive for mission? There does not appear to be anything that has taken the place of yesterday's passion for souls. We almost appear to be in a twilight period where one imperative has lost its power and others have not yet emerged. Perhaps this is why the compelling urgency which led to such deeds of courage and faithfulness is no longer present. A new motive for evangelism is urgently required. I suggest it will be not a single imperative, but a multiple motive, that will sustain a new evangelism.

The reality of God can be the beginning of mission. Being truly human means responding to the transcendent, the spiritual dimension of life. We are all made for fellowship with God. People who miss this are only half-alive and are doomed to a shallow and superficial, even supercilious, existence.

To present God as a living presence relevant to life today can be a dominant motive for mission. In this rather distorted period when the churches have too often allowed the world to write the agenda of its task, when we have succumbed to a so-called secular gospel, the significance of the transcendent has faded.

I remember the editor of an Australian newspaper saying to me one day: "I cannot understand the church now. The Christian church is surely supposed to major on God; people are hungry for God, and the church gives the impression of talking about everything but God."

Social service, social action, counseling, and group

12